# BESIEGE ME

Book Cover Art: c.pic_, *Untitled* (2020). Courtesy of the Artist.
Book Cover Design: Alban Fischer
Book Interior Design: Sarah Gzemski

Published by Noemi Press, Inc. A Nonprofit Literary Organization.
www.noemipress.org.

NICHOLAS WONG

# BESIEGE

# ME

# CONTENTS

# CHILDREN OF CHINA

We wake, forced to taste
your colostrum. The table is
set with a sanctity of humans
locking up humans. Outside,
the Great Wall. So great that
we've grown into the
efficient teeth of sprockets.
Plackets, rockets, & luck,
you replicated. Of course,
came cash. We spent its
slipperiness. *Time has taught
you I'm the world's biggest
stakeholder*, you said. The
fact is, you're aimlessly loud
& lewd—in a gallery or
gulch, squatting. *Exaggerate
until they accept you*, you
said. In China, more foot
masseuses than feet. More
eye surgeons than witnesses.
That is to say, *more* is
orgasmic. Your tanks broke
the humerus to write
humorous music in 1989.
Another fact. *It isn't funny,*
you said, *because funny only
applies to things I admit have
happened.* No wonder each
face looks mugwort-dull
when the anthem plays.

"The city is currently a faulty immune system."

John Yau


"I mean as the world, a potential of matter and light, but I speak of it obliquely
as young men and possibilities I imagine for romance."

Mei-mei Berssenbrugge

# INTERGENERATIONAL

When you gave a few pushes on my mom
to give me manhood & a prostate, you also
gave me a natal chart & some bones to break
in the years of fire. Maybe I *feet head no good*
(brought bad luck). Still, I was given a surface
to be licked by teenage tongues I then knew
was called skin. A face I couldn't put away
fast enough to avoid mistakes. Then you sold
your yellow Beetle, told me *yellow* is a homonym
of your last name & mine. There's no gold.
I forgot how you parented yourself. Should I decide
it for you? At immigration, I clarified that people
like us had last names first & first names last.
I gathered balled socks from home for the hospital.
I heard you say *please* in bed. You left your beans
on the plate as if to contemplate the history
of beans. I liked how you said *lei ah yeah*
(your grandpa) not as a familial reference, but to curse.
*No good my lungs lei ah yeah*, you said.
Then I remembered viruses in cartoons always
looked irregular. Curses were an immodest
form of childhood; curse at your own
risk. Then, clear your phlegm, clear
your phlegm, clear your phlegm. You still
didn't ask about the men I brought home,
so I didn't tell you I was sisterly polyphagic.
TV said K Pop was a happy virus & males
got pregnant in the seahorse world. So much
phlegm thickens in your lungs. You took
your pills when I watched animal programs
& learned that survival was hierarchical.
Ugly fish were often accompanied by "Oriental
music," while dolphins swam in an ocean
of orchestra. Then you cleared your phlegm,
cleared it & it. You asked why I pulled out tissues
from a paper box as if from the center of you.

# FIRST MARTYR

"Many among the vast crowds... carried white flowers tributes to an anonymous man who had fallen to his death the previous evening after unfurling a large protest banner on scaffolding near government headquarters."
—*The Guardian* on the Anti-Extradition Bill Movement, Hong Kong, 2019.

Hello, white flowers. Hello, origami swans.

One of you is alive; the other, more so.

A caterpillar dies for its arithmetic smallness.

Hello, stinky times. Hello, rhapsodic feet. Now I have more swans

than ponds, prayers than pain. Hello, hymns

in D-flat minors, ribbons interwoven as if wishing badly to begin.

Cheer up—isn't *bad* a moving process relative to power?

The candles lit across the street, a grip.

Until we're caught, expand the protest route.

Remember the sweat & jeering wind. I hope

my head didn't look like a savaged plum in the news.

My vantage flipped my fear. Sweet violence—

I saw through it. This world, always slow in its giving.

# APOLOGY TO A BESIEGED CITY

If I scattered dug-out bricks to stop the water cannons.

If I swung teargas canisters back to the cops with a squash racket.

If I wasn't a sheep in a milder herd.

If toddlers weren't taught to draw a unicorn—then remove its horn, call it a horse.

If elders weren't trained as gamecocks, plucking each other's eyes with berserk beaks.

If all windows were taken away so no one would see if there's a cloud
      over the world, another sun behind the cloud.

If you weren't still resisting the anti-bliss of the double rainbow.

If fire didn't become the unit of currency for a briefness.

If I didn't empty my wallet.

If I didn't dare the flames to groom the hours themselves.

# ADVICE FROM A PRO-BEIJING LOBBYIST

The best geh way to show faith in the Communist Party is to wait
until dusk loh. The night seals your urge for independence.
The sun isn't omnipotent ga. It kowtows to the party in day
broad light. The Red Guards are friendly; no need scare lah.
Their hands grow a hemlock, penis big as a cicada's leg.
When they serve people lei they say, *Try my breast.*
Whether or not to take it literally jau you can decide gei.
See? There's freedom. It's okay ga to like Americans
like SpongeBob, so long as you also find ways to caulk
the sky until the city furls in discipline, dry from serrated
democrats & the shape of floods gum loh. By the fuck,
what the way, why're you thinking? No need to think lah.
Keep your head light like flounce; our leader is charming
like a Tic-Tac. Your knife dou no need la. You'll be utterly safe.
Plus, the blade is thantophobic. We'll be comrades ma.
You ask ask others la. Comrades love each other so much,
the campaign posters look homoerotic. Don't take it the other way lah—
two rods clanging isn't rhapsodic. Sameness shouldn't
be allowed in sex. I know, you people worry this & that
yau mud yau mud. We care about human rights as much
as we do about the Johnny Depp scandal. Those we arrest, we arrest
because their eyes are hollow of morning sparkle.
We want our people to glow, but not brighter than the Party.
No, ears aren't treason. Speech isn't erasure. The media
turns fetid & white as it gets old. If alphabets are votes,
the most democratic word is *pneumonoultramicroscopicsilico-*
*volcanoconiosis.* Say it in a breath, as if knowing what it means.

# BIASED BIOGRAPHY OF MY FATHER

A man who jerked in parked lorries
at the age of 12 & slept there,
whose dreams didn't raise him,
who bullied himself into the realm
of pharmaceuticals, whose boss said
*Apprentice. Ape. You.*, who navigated
the pain of A-words (Aspirin, Alpain,
Advanced White, Amen), who acted
knowing these words inside-
out, whose acting imitated plastic
imitating glass, who turned the corner
of his adolescence like that & bragged
about the turn, whose brag was the man
was his wound, whose wounds
are public & his palms never a poetic
domain, who was warned by palmists
about having three children (among
whom one is not to be discussed),
who pledged to be reread,
who realized manhood was bringing rice
to bowls & wearing mortgage
as daily work clothes, who missed dinners,
who missed most of his kids' childhoods
busy selling cough syrup, who coughed
& felt the back of his lungs
hard like a board, whose name meant
*moon-owning* or *happy friends,* whose name lacked
the theatrics like *Marlon Brando* or *Al Pacino,*
who found the cinematic mafia's way of gambling
so compelling he doubled the hit-hit-
split, who's obsessed with the swift incision
of occasional winning, who scattered options
& defeat across a table so they looked
manageable, who studied the odds
& the struts of getting *it* right, whose dice
the queen hated to toss, who tumbled to live
linearly, whose life, accordingly, concurred.

# THE LITTLE PINK

In praise of the regime, I
seal my cravings in latex gloves.
In hard times, they become

firm pressure balls I squeeze.
In praise of the firewall that illuminates
my perspective. I see it now

as an intersection for the disturbed
penis & Pornhub. In praise of pre-selecting
my food. Every bite, an education holding my soul

strong against foreign powers, which, as I convince
my friends, are relentless as sand fleas.
In praise of cutting scenes of teenage loves.

Instead, the young should etch language into
cuttlefish, hummingbirds, & GDP.
Our ocean. Our sky. Our land.

# DARK ADAPTATION

In the year 2052, poets will be in great demand in Hong Kong because of Cultural Revolution 2.0, which will eliminate Cantonese and popular cultural texts produced in the language. After much stress-induced sex, a number of bilingual poets will preserve Cantopop songs by means of homophonic translation.

Some of the poets involved in this "Dark Adaptation" project will be arrested or *be disappeared* (note the passive voice intentionally used together with an active verb to suggest involuntary behavior). They will not be charged with treason or advocating overthrow of the government. They will, instead, be charged with not complying with the duty of being writers, which, in their government's feeling, is to provide closed yet didactic meanings. The following poem is the last piece the poets will write before they *are disappeared*. Their readers are to complete the blanks.

This is how it was in the beginning: some eggs knew
what to do with _____ if _____ did not break them.

It was always a battle between the _____
& the _____ that kept rising behind the door.

A grand law about _____ was hatched fast
enough but was hated even faster.

You woke up emptied of _____
A. Chicken    B. Chicken    C. Chicken.

You hoped _____, not _____, could win
a perfect problem.

Someone was saying something about
A. _____      B. _____      C. Emotional pedagogy of road signs.

A flame burning with _____ was a proof of dissent.
No beginning cared about destiny or duration.

Water poured into a _____ that had not been dug,
one had to _____.

_____ was a psychic on the road.
In a city you pointed from, you pointed at the city—

The one that was emptied in someone's fist of _____.
The one where you had been taught not to _____.

You were a _____ in a cavern, walking
through years between *just do it* & *you did it*.

# 101, TAIPEI

You're here early. Shouldn't you be going home, where questions
are decades old? The ones you are expecting won't come—
the star barista, the edgy clerk, the entrepreneur who burns
family photos. Do you know the 21st century took your belongings inside?
To be exact with the price of a thing (a rooster plate, a rope),
add 99 cents to its worth to make its value feel more real. You wonder
what the steel of my 101st floor is for. To you, am I still the same
meetup spot & torque that yanks you toward a man's center, or just a phallus?
I have become a witness standing by your loneliness. All winter long,
a raw anticipation aches. Everyone in this city crawls toward everyone
less sad-looking now. Some come with their cameras to frame
the circumference of their open despair. It's conservative to say
only the natural world matters. I'm famous. I appear in maps.
Didn't you come for a city view sped up by happiness? Now, jump.
The body bag isn't plastic art—it's in the zip.

# ON INSERTION

I'm now fluid-
conscious, though still

called riffraff
by those who fuss

about crises
between the legs.

I put on my shoes
to expose a spine

of cursed commas.
I like the pain

I cause to glossed
leather when I tug

the shoelaces. Aren't
our bodies a pair

of rotating blades
that carve the love

out of us? Tell me
how often I'm wanted

like clean laundry.
Nothing less

than a multi-entered
porn star, collared

between *in love* & *in
addition to this love.*

# I SWIPE MY AMEX TO COVER MY FATHER'S TREATMENT FOR A VIRUS IN HIS LUNG I DON'T KNOW HOW TO PRONOUNCE

At the hospital, we've become
entrepreneurs of standing around.
My head's spinning like an agitator.
My point being, in comparison,
you're a black hole.
My _____-ness can't be spoken
of like my salary. We should, but can't
talk about my nights that involve
many limbs. I think _____ thoughts,
play _____ chess, walk _____ dogs.
*I'm bored & proud*, you say.
Even then, I knew you knew it.
When the virus stippled your lungs,
I imagined you asking me why I read
Sartre. I imagined you saying,
*You aren't like me.* True,
my _____ shadow ruffles
on your burdock-reeking torso,
& my lungs aren't shadowed,
computed, invoiced, item
by item, then saved & paid
for, then turned into redeemable
mileage, mane, & deer fences
I pretend feel exotic
in numerous selfies to pay
the filial debts of my _____ skin.
You remain beside me
like a receipt. Years later, will someone
say, *True* when I say what you've said?
Without leaving me alone to feel
the being & depletion
of being _____?

# VACUUM

According to Amnesty International, in 2013, there were 319,325 migrant workers in Hong Kong:

"[A]bout half were Indonesian and nearly all were women... Recruitment and placement agencies, in Indonesia and Hong Kong respectively, are routinely involved in the trafficking of migrant workers and their exploitation in conditions of forced labor."

## 0. SITUATIONS

The moon blue, shy to know you at first,
now asks for your childhood spoon.
Its edge & back once mashed a world

into paste for your mouth, which
has learned about survival. Later,
you know habits form territories.

You choose to sweat in Hong Kong streets,
eat take-out with chopsticks that don't split
like win-win situations.


## 1. ENTRANCE

It takes a romantic to say extroverts need a large world
to perch on love.

You run to look for the cause—
why a clock loses its hands to get to time,
while time crushes continuity.

You have a new ma'am who visits the salon
every Saturday for the same soufflé hairdo.

You want to adjust time, but it adjusts others.

Everybody surrenders in the same way.
Leave your arms at the entrance.


## 2. YOURS

A cobra imitates a collar & says constraint is fine
so long as it's gentle.

How hard does forgiveness scratch?

Humpback whales are mammalian jukeboxes.
Each song is twenty minutes long.

How long do your regrets last if you keep them
in a tight jar with herbs that aren't even yours?


## 3. IT

At first, [   ] didn't have any friends in this strange place.
At first, [   ] insisted on the use of Cantonese because—

[   ] was anxious about not living

up to the expectations of society. At first,
[   ] had another home, the home with _____.

At first, [   ] would rather not use *them* to refer to
those who used *them* to refer to her
& people like her.

At first, he, who [   ] called *Sir*, disliked [   ].

Labor, at first, could be sustained
if his hands avoided [   ] in this three-bedroom apartment—
before [   ] avoided narrating it.


## 4. MACHINE

The placenta, a script for loneliness.

If the night is blood, the day wades.

I wake to a delayed language.

A slaughter of nouns to select colors.
Flags are an assertion of disheveling winds.

My medical record is clean, no allergy.
I got bitten by your city's teeth.
Shall I declare my prayers, safety pins, & childhood crush?

*These cams are watching you if your hands open things*
*they shouldn't,* Ma'am said.

She didn't know that he—the one who picked me—
had already filmed me. He saw my fingers between my legs.

I have two legs like some sockets.
When he pressed the vacuum cleaner's tube into my mouth,
I was just a make-happy machine.

I made him a happier machine.


## 5. DO

*Wash Grandma before chemo. Don't frown.*
*I've seen you. Buy your own bowl. The table*
*is for us. You eat by the stove.*

*No Jesus behind this door. We're Buddhists.*
*I've seen you. Don't leave the tap running.*
*Don't run. I keep your passport.*

*No Skyping your sisters at night. No night*
*is yours. Don't switch your tone. Don't*
*switch on the Wi-Fi yourself. I've seen you.*

*Don't act like a man with your boots on Sundays.*
*I've seen you. Don't kiss your friends. They're friends.*
*We're family. There are things lips shouldn't do.*

## 6. EXPLAIN—

| | | finally became a subject.
Or an event.

Her lips slightly parted
for a fearful language
to emerge.

A neighborhood
dipped in small talks: *should have...*
*if not... I saw it*
*coming.*

Some went on with a vagueness.
Some saw her head (from a newspaper
or in person): purpled, swollen.

*Explain how it happened,*
the police asked, as if the self were the cause
for the force. The force,

then an object
the force imposed upon.
So go on. Explain—

## 7. ALONE

Alone in the sitting room, so much to dust.
I neared the window, the jagged skyline.
What if demolition is the true form
of permanence? A nest is a storm in drag.

My family don't live with me anymore.
Things are either *are* or *aren't.*

Happiness is a notion that rejects
pretending. I corrected my texture to fit in.

Furniture has a reputation of being hard.
Why did people still ask why I acted like a countertop?


## 8. WHEN

When the police made me sit in this room for hours
& my victimhood stood behind a motive
that didn't exist, my vocabulary reached

an end. The world had changed.
The wind started a trend, under which we all had to prove
we're innocent.

Something strange when they copied what I said.
No crossing out allowed, otherwise the report
would have no legal standing.

They tried to rewrite my language,
so that a certain truth could be constructed.

My instinct told me there's evidence
to prove that some colors got devoured.

But those eyes, concerned with accuracy,
looked at mine, as if my third eye showed.

## Re: Work (Interruption 1)

Hit Man Gurung, *I Have To Feed Myself, My Family and My Country*
(2013, acrylic on printed canvas).


In a story, a girl lets loose
a balloon. No one blames
its motion when it bursts.

Like the first stanza, the second
begins with the speaker talking
about her head, its past,

how she was forced to give it up,
how she overcame it with other
headless sisters—her BFF's.

BFF: Bartered For Fortune.
A head for a house, a pink
schoolbag of dirt.

When her head exploded,
she was in rags, in *a crowd
of thighs without occupation.*

On the back of each note,
a headshot of some men, meaning
iPhones & clothes sent

back home. Adding "your head"
to sentences means denial, a scoff,
in Cantonese: *Holiday your head.*

*Dignify your head.*

## 9. DAYS

[    ] went on explaining:

> I matured in the first month
> after arrival. I babysat.
> I kept quiet, out of sight.
> I didn't dream.
> I readied. I reacted.
> My back arched.
> I repelled.
> *The body is self-rewarding.*
> *This may take a few days.*

## 10. DUST

*Match an image below with A MAID,*
says the kid's homework. Flip-flops,
clogged pores. My made-ness makes his home work.

The kid calls me *eight woman.* He says
if I enough ginger, I can talk back.
Grandma eats chips behind Ma'am.

She murmurs, *fry squid* if I *report string.*
If I triple my strength, I dare they *have teeth.*
Ten years ago, I left home to *do the world.*

I *see road carefully, face green green, walk walk*
*stand stand,* a day is gone.
I *have seeds* that grow into debts that are sewn
into a fence. Behind it, I thin myself to contradict dust.

## Re: Work (Interruption 2)

Sun Yuan & Peng Yu, *Hong Kong Intervention* (2009/2016, digital prints on paper).


Tonight, a pin slips
off a grenade. An explosion
quick, but grand.

In this home, where
you're free to weave
between the public lives

of clothes & their hanging,
you put feculent love-
grenades above a freezer,

a cooker, on four mats.
Most nights, the ritual
of *cannot not* leaves a hole

also in you, despite the slow
power of double denials.
The name for the shoe

of a shoeshine boy isn't Shoe.
Your brain scattering
its fictional mess at a metro stop

isn't called Brain. What
naming does is easy.
It doesn't speak of agony.

## 11. Q

Q: Do you know first aid?
[ ]: I keep words in the fridge. They rot at room temperature.

Q: Shall we start a list somewhere of bad maids?
[ ]: What is *bad?* I defrost my words at the mountaintop.

Q (insisting): This one talks back.
[ ]: When language reaches the trough, the wind looks for a reddened face,
     or an anemone, or anyone.

Q (acting sympathetic): Let her go.
[ ] (in a confessing tone): I, by mistake, fried a gourd with a gourd. But my cooking skills
     are more than purely a matter of gourd-ness.

[ ] (with surfacing anxiety): Problem is, I've been thinking a lot about space. I mean, I'm
     longer than my bed. When space dies, should my understanding of my body go with it?

Q (with a plotted abusive intent): Now bend over.
[ ] (worried about her contract): When I tell you I'm not adjustable like you patella band,
     you say there's a saying: *Be nice.*

Q (aside):  They are things we live among. Seeing them is like seeing scattered clothes hangers.
     We have to think about what to do with them.


## 12. [ ] REMEMBERS

[ ] remembers her agency once asked her
how she disciplined children, to which she should
have answered: *They are things we live among.*

*Seeing them is like seeing scattered clothes hangers.*
*I think about what to do with them.*

   *This one talks back.*

## 13. AWAY

Away from home means the definition
of friendship changes into a love
hotel I check into every other Sunday.

She says, *Your eyes focus faster than you think.*

*There are things that operate only with distance.*
Noise.
*Echo.*
Away.
*Home.*
My hand.
*In mine.*


## 14. STAND

I'm not the personified water spider
from a children's book, didn't start tiny,
like a burnt chestnut. I wasn't given

a narrative arc, or few glossy pages
of transformation. I'm not the ninja
on page 4. The creature skittering across

the pond isn't my kitsch. My original self
isn't a sunken collapsible boat.
Not hyperbole, or a pet you & the city

agreed to keep after a one-night stand.

# Re: Work (Interruption 3)

Elvis Yip Kin Bon, *If You Miss Home* (2016, single-channel video).


This is your cultural capital speaking
shrouded in mosaics, timed
by a video. What will

you do? *Think, I will, the future
of my son.* Your melancholy
is overbooked. We ask you to focus.

To practice... *bridge is falling down.*
Downed ownership: What if
you miss your family?

*I will keep myself busy.* Focus,
adjusted, falling down. But self—
*AH!*—This is your cultural

capital speaking. Your self
is sublingual. *Kalua tidak bobo.*
If you aren't sleeping well, odd

yourself out. Notion of self
in English only, such as *wood and clay
will wash away.* It's humanity's

interest to have verbs come first:
done work, bear this. We don't speak
much of diasporas here. Though seared,

focus. *Even iron bars will bend
and break.* What will you do
if you break? *Photos. Wrinkles.*

*Blender.* Remember no one
expects shoes to clean themselves.
*AH!*—To make sure you're employable,

answer this. What's worse than falling:
a floor that cants, or one that can't refuse what falls?

# DARK ADAPTATION

As the song title assembles, the road, one that's been
outlasted, calls for a tune that sings of, if you must,
one thing—young men of luck choking on unknowns.
Their boots, full of holes, whiny eyebrows sinking,
their eyes have been taken for repair. Now, everyone
claims it's fine to kill a boy in a hole so long as that
hole is a toy made by a law, & the law by the
misinterpretation of another law. The night hisses
in red. Everyone looks for a sound to tell the worst
harmless joke. Taunt a hand by the sea, neat rows of
boats can't wipe off the wind to understand the
cackling of leaving home, & that their return,
sometimes, happens by mistake.

# SELF-PORTRAIT AS MY BOYFRIEND'S ROLEX

He wanted to be thought
of as all that's left & left
with, with more PrEP
& monologues of strange
proteins. Your first date
with him—looking back,
would your face change
if you already knew?
Then, in his car, seats
reclined, you kissed the curve
of his thumb, sniffed
his hair scented with work.
He told you how he raged
at the hospital triage: *Cheap fucks*
*took my watch.* How he became
a human sugar cube in meth-
parties. You felt like windshield
wipers made to clear glass
underwater. He said, *It's not*
*like I wanted it.* It took your
hand some time to touch his
trembling wrist, rub my
crystal face. Admit it:
you like it, too. The bare
erotics of denial.

# GRINDR

I asked the government to seal my urn
with pure coal, but they never acknowledged

my fetish for hands. My life so far:
mostly shells scrimshawing me.

The economy thwacks
me bruise-less. I look for someone

to not discuss politics—
who stops endorsing people like us.

A serious rainbow lover.
Like it with the lights off.

Like it more when a man nods
in the dark, denying

that one of us is nodding.
Tend to discover whatever lurches

under the tongue is a dungeon.
Tested negative after I climbed

over my father to hone
the daggers between our eyes.

# NATIONALISM IS A TOTE BAG I USE EVERY DAY

Its strap, capable
of strangers.
I wear it cross-bodily
for evening occasions:
dolphin planks
at the gym, penetrating
random men.
The tote morphs.
It starts calling
itself high fashion.
Its ego opens holes
to lose my keys
every time I join a protest.
I find myself huddling
in the tote to make
space for the designer's
expectations—uphold
faith in the Three Gorges Dam,
retract my condemning
tongue as walls of stones
collapse. At home,
the sight of it repulses
me. I say, *we live together,*
*but we live far apart.*
To stop thoughts
about my divided home,
I sleep. But some nights,
beads keep falling between
the walls, & I remember
a story about communists
who flick marbles before stitching
their love marks on our lips.

# FIVE ACTS WITH FATHER

### I.

If, like the saying goes, we were lovers
in a previous life and that makes us
father & son in this one, perhaps
I didn't love you enough.

### II.

I could have chosen your sex.
*How?*
Like Grandpa choosing your name.
*You think so?*
Like choosing an enemy.

### III.

I petrified my secrets.
*About what?*
You know what.
*Where do your sins go?*
The neck. No difficulty at all.

### IV.

Remember your first spoken word?
*Father.*
Like affliction?
*Also like a wish.*

### V.

No wishing. To each wish, a wing.
*The word flies when spoken.*
No, it crawls.
*That's your ideal, just upside down.*
That's my idea of you.

# BIASED BIOGRAPHY OF MY MOTHER

```
                                    to
the         of                              &
to the          I              to        their
                up with              over its
to      my              about their
                              to them. In the
        彡 彡 of                  乂 彳
a       from                          over a
over                    that          in
                  I    her
to      out             the              before I
its         I                    in the         the
to      her             in
        she      to            after    that
                        her
into                    an        of
that          the                      with
I      about that        because
            toward a      of                        a
        I            of my              when she's
        out before I              up     a     of
from        apart or      that        behind
            I              myself the      of        the
but I   it        to                that she      the
        with      to      with
by              & to      as            on his
                        I
of her      in my              the          she
        because she          in it
A       isn't the            of            so
    I      the          between the              by
I          my                  over a
which I          or        I              with
that                  I              her then if
```

# GOLDEN

**01**

Despite what all linguists have said, you have to agger
that the goodest English
is the *identity of our physical forms*

Or that it *is banal between lovers but it is not that*

**02**

It is pretentious / 煩膠
to begin a poem with quotes
from Mei-mei Berssenbrugge or Anne Carson

**03**

Why? They're serious poets

Because 認真就輸了

**04**

回帶 : The goodest English
is *delights on egos*

**05**

Now that we have laid the foundation
that poetry is about playfulness
let's move forward

Agger

**06**

Since June, two hordes of beasts
are in conflict with each other

One accuses the other, *You've made a living seam*
The other defends, *That's a living sail*


## 07
中出 is what seems to be a solution

A middle exit a neutral exit a potential of witness and intent


## 08
(A group of 左膠 nods)


## 09
Neutrality is not a compromise
The former is a disguise for one's missing
bells of shame

Compromise is like remorse reflected
in a shop's window,
exposing yourself to an affair that way


## 10
Aren't you worried
*No*
Aren't you worried about those guys
*No*
Aren't you worried that those guys came but had to sit alone
*Yes*


## 11
Companionship is as comforting
as applesauce (fact-checked)


## 12
Though my arms my butt my guts

are not J-able as those of the 巴打
on the front line

They take notice of me and my requests


13
Teach me HTML
Teach me how to sleep

The nights have stopped
their wrangle of rationality


14
To justify my hehe FF, allow me to bring in Bruce Lee


15
He once said, *If nothing within you stays*
*rigid, outward things will disclose themselves*

& *water can flow or it can crash*
(So, #bewater, my friend)


16
One of those quotes is suspiciously homosocial

As in quote 巳 J
As in J 巳 cut
As in cut 巳 done
As in done 巳 done


17
When a narrative ends, be the hacksaw
or hacksaw-ready

**18**

Not all water wants to drown
The plain one just wants to spill


**19**

The city's walls & streets will soon grow
immune to bullets invented & not

啪啪啪啪啪啪啪啪啪啪啪啪啪啪啪


**20**

Take a voluble selfie with someone's spinal ink

# CITY MESS, MOTHER MESS, FLUIDS MESS

Umbrella Revolution, Hong Kong

An umbilical cord grows after it's cut.
A kind of moving-on, a swerve.

                              I disclose my distress
                              but my tongue can't thin
                              the pain of the unrest's song.

The year Margaret Thatcher was elected, she was elected.
The year Margaret Thatcher was elected, people began panic-buying oil.
The year Margaret Thatcher was elected, history was tossed.
That she was elected tussled with my city's umbilical cord.

        A swerving.
        The year Margaret Thatcher was elected, I was born.

*This is how you're captured—a crude silhouette,*
said my childhood.


I was 6. My mother moved me to an elite school,
where my ears were incised by new grammar, new words.

She handled my homework with dread—
larva, disarm, karma.


I once spelled *grammar* as *grammer*, grimmer, rim.

Mother wanted me to study pharmacy, but I dated a DJ
thick with beat-boxing tricks instead.
A medley. A joint. A white mantis imitating a tulip.


Then she handled me with dread, as if she knew the rest
of my life would be spent rewarding men who open their legs to me.


Twenty years of being a body feast.
Larva: restrained flowers.
Disarm: luck off a hook.
Karma: bets upon bets.


*Accuracy? Go on, then—*
*to write about the tragedy of this body.*

Mother's crying record (mostly during phone calls).

Call 1: sister's lesbianism/the self-deluded bliss
        that I was not *one of them.*
Call 2 (from sister): *I mean... bliss.*
Call 3: Grandma fell in a nursing home.
Call 4 (from hospital): Grandma choked on her own feces, her body
        medically an *it.* The feces had to find a way to leave *it.*
        Her mouth was the only opening.
Call 5: *One of them* slept over. A newish toothbrush tilts
        against a basin, awash with the spit of two men.

To fragment is to steadily lay down what memory allows. Fragmenting as drilling,
attempting to re-know. They get things done.

I have problems sleeping.
*A kiss is not a way to focus.*

In my head, a body mess: the year Margaret Thatcher was elected,
if my mother's womb held me longer, I'd have had a natal chart
guaranteeing me a lifetime of luck. *But you already got me*
*in labor for eight hours.*

The Iron Lady fell on the stairs outside the Great Hall of the People in China.

In my head, the men whose bushes I'd rather shave than rush home for dinner.

My ex-boyfriend named his marketing campaign
LED BY HER. *The phrase is in the public*
*domain. Free for use.*

His campaign was my longest relationship with women
other than my mother.

In pharmacy, $A_B$
I)      tells the amount of drugs in the body.
II)     infers replacing A with *Mother*, B with *Me*.
III)    II, and Mother$_{Me}$ looks like 孕.
IV)     all of the above.

Lately, I often find threads (彡 彡) of her hair crisscrossing (乂 犭) in the icebox, as if
I)      they're taking a break from housework.
II)     she deliberately left them in the fridge.
III)    I had to care for her (Me$_{Mother}$).
IV)     none of the above. (There is no Chinese character for this role-flip.)

Even if there were such a character (Me$_{Mother}$), I know I wouldn't
I)      adhere to what it meant.
II)     give up wanting my own home, my own financial security.
III)    stop wanting to cash out my parents for a down payment.
IV)     avoid feeling trapped living with them.

Not knowing what to do, I distance myself emotionally from
I)      her.
II)     him.
III)    all of the above.

I feel like I have to
I)      ravage this expensive city.
II)     find myself a sugar daddy.
III)    flatten a piece of paper I have crumpled in a rage, back to its perfect form.
IV)     come to terms with self-blame.

*Fluids today seem terrifying—a departure*
I admit I would play with his fluids until *he* lasts.

Maybe, I'm one of those children who inevitably turn
out to be wasteful, like all other children?

"The Sino-British Joint Declaration is a treaty between the United Kingdom and China on
Hong Kong under Chinese sovereignty. [It was] signed by Chinese Premier Zhao Ziyang
and UK Prime Minister Margaret Thatcher on behalf of their respective governments...
Hong Kong's way of life would be unchanged for 50 years until 2047."

Only umbrellas. No rain.
The news that students were crushed
like strudel, pepper-sprayed in the face
& on wrinkling raincoats.

Imagine this home that is lessened, moves on
with *without*. Without signs
of lives: choices, autonomy, hairs.

Weeks ago, my mother cried over a loneliness,
over her hunch that my father, in his mid-seventies,
was seeing someone else. *It's someone
from work.* Her sorrow so raw that I didn't know
how to react. I shut my room door.
Our home is small, like mercies.

My heart jagged like an escalator step.
23 likes to my post, *Police about to shoot.*

When the mouth of a gun points at a face that looks
like the gun holder's face, it is not hatred but politics.

Subjects to avoid at the dinner table:
- the streets uncertainly filled
- democracy or pissoir
- strangers with skin ready to be contrived

I trash expired foods in the fridge to make more space. Pasta sauce in stained jars, chicken essence cubes that look like rock-hard caramel candies my mother's teeth can no longer bite into. I erase these traces of her when she's crying her eyes out, before I realize her stocking up is a means of trying to keep things from falling apart.

The crowd dispersed eastward to occupy
another site when I arrived.

At a junction, a man passed me plastic wrap & wet towels.
I looked at his hand, which I also wanted.

*If no one should bring deceit into duty,*
*you should not bring your penis to the protest.*

A hyper-real Shiseido billboard
hollered *No Defects* above me.

My arrival felt approved
by the swoosh on my shoes.

The street, *long as patience.*
*In a crowd, ego did not exist.*

History & students maneuver at the door.

*Both reaching to open it saying "excuse me"*
*Passing through together saying "excuse me"*
*Both reaching to close it saying "excuse me"*
*Backing in reverse to the door both reaching to open it saying "after you"*
*Passing through together both reaching to close it saying "after you"*
*Locating four more doors and repeating*
*Still another door*

"In December 2013, the toy became a symbol of opposition to the Hong Kong government, after an incident during a town hall event where a Lufsig was thrown by a protester at [named redacted], the Chief Executive, who had been nicknamed 'the wolf' by his critics. Following the incident [and the discovery that its transliterated Chinese name sounds similar to 'motherfucker' when pronounced in Cantonese], Lufsig experienced a surge in popularity, selling out at IKEA stores in Hong Kong, as well as in several outlets in mainland China."

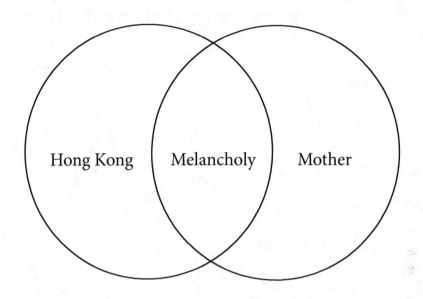

Rationales for melancholy:

1. "China uses Hong Kong's currency, equity and debt markets to attract foreign funds, while international companies use Hong Kong as a launchpad to expand into mainland China."
2. Use: to consume. Mother as a launchpad. Each morning, she slices apricot bread & makes my father an oatmeal. She demands a kiss on her chin before he goes to work.
3. Use. Use. Us: to put into gluttony, like a sword venturing deeper & deeper into the swallower's throat until the rain-guard kisses his lips.
4. Her life after marriage has been task-based. She is pronouns, prepositions, & connectives.
5. Her systolic pressure today: 173.

The police clarified they had no intention
to shoot. Clarified to shoot. Intended
to clarify. To shoot. Had no intention
to clarify. To shoot the police. The intended.


During a site clearing, a woman was convicted
of pumping her breasts on a cop's arm.

To kill absurdity, aim at its head.

If it has no head, then kill its habitat.

But I can't kill my home, where it feels good for me to be hollow
& hollowed out like the *who* in *whoever.*

A drum's skin mounted to a rim
near my throat.

The rain is a misnomer of the weather.
One umbrella, two, three thousand
& more make a day.

My trembling myringa
implies *respond* is my favorite word.
But *responsible* has a weight—
a tightrope walker choosing
which side to fall, midair.

What cities & bodies deny a sometimes-crisis,
not knowing they're a series of which?

The teargas is beauty, puked after a long night.

The city's brain is broken, its stem alive.
Nothing emptier beats emptying.

*Can you be shockproof?* I ask language.
Waylaid, it arcs away—its last spark.
Not the brightest, but the one cuing smartly: a cry.

# DARK ADAPTATION

A hole is digging itself at home, knowing I want a second home. Deep inside, I find a son that I'll never have—the one that I've always tied up. He looks like a damaged chime, leaning toward the wind. Most mornings, there are imperfect sounds—though not as imperfect as my name, its sound imposed onto me. That's how the world has known me. No one sings anymore. It's replaced by waiting for a second home. Waiting has become an expertise. Everyone looks for thumbprints in each other's secrets. Each hand has five pins. I hold up my son to let him see the skyline.

# YOUTH (AS PREDICTED)

Words passed like music
in my teenage years: *lips,*

*hoax, pry.* More
often than not, too many lips

endlessly opened as I got
posey, as if pivoting

on a pommel horse.

◆

*Are you the one*, the doctor asked,
*who "received" or "gave"?*

His gown, half-
curing & half-suspicious,

sculpted a version
of me into binary.

◆

*Beneath the skin of a king,*
*a wolf.*

Before the lovers appeared
standing on the card,

they furrowed the earth,
composted it with allegories.

# INVITATION

If I tell you the floral arch is my body & whose hands they are, would you come to the wedding? I can't explain my choice, or why there are excitement-bright nipples on the arch. You've met him. His hands are sometimes borders, sometimes the world to me. I'm scared of carrying on, because I know exactly when the day breaks. I know what you mean when you say *knowing less is a blessing*. I want you to know more. He still kneels beside me until a word places itself in my heart. It's my heart that knows when the day breaks. The day watches him pause & he watches me weigh apologies. I'm scared. We spent the past few months measuring confessions & secrets. The world is an extension cord. You didn't tell me each lover is born with a sweet tooth & they fold their sadness inwards. You didn't tell me a wedding is to undo a reasonable split. Would you come? We'll invite 唐綺陽, 張君雅, & our mothers. Would you still come if we have a fast-food theme for catering? Jollibee, McNuggets, & other lichen-like shit, so the guests can't register the contrast of their first & second plates? I can't explain my choice. I once spread myself as wide as possible to increase the catchment area for falling in love. I can't explain. When I met him, he cooked for me. We're thinking of inviting 阿妹 & going live on IG (#連名帶姓 #soundbite). Are you scared? We can leave you out of the frame, but bring an extension cord to our wedding. You've met him, but I didn't tell you our late supper at 小李子, or that Taipei rebuilt us. I didn't tell you we didn't need to bear the strength of each passing eye, while holding hands in 仁愛路. Did I scare you? Still, bring an extension cord. I can't explain my choice. I no longer want my life emptied like the space inside a highball glass. With him, I want to see a hive of light coiling & hear its tinkling sound. With him, I know how I feel & want to feel the knowing. Is the velocity of these wants too much? You can't explain my choice, either. Sometimes, it's hurtful to see we're barefaced & resplendent. Sometimes, people like us dress up as clowns to say hello to strangers. I wish you told me what drives a wedding. An act of faith? I wish you told me intimacy could be a floral arch, just installed. Are you scared if I'm not? What if I tell you I want you to be there? Say yes. I'll stop re-telling my story so carefully, I promise.

# SEEKING PATERNAL GUIDANCE ON ABSENCES

In *Happy Together* (1997): an absence of women,
but maternity spawns at the inseam of Iguazu Falls.

○

That hole water rages into is a lack nursing alluvial lust.

○

*Too Freudian. Rephrase, so your father can understand it.*

○

FLASHFORWARD: Post-screening Q&A.
Would my father give rustling responses,
*The film sounds moist. / Is it a humid porn?*

○

FLASHBACK: My childhood crosscutting
fragments of Saturday movie nights in the '80s.

A montage of Jackie Chan's stunts, in-mall jumps
& compulsion to show his buttocks as a comic relief.

○

Back then, our popcorn-dried lips
made a generation-gulf. We spoke less.

○

Gradually less about the necessity of women
in plots, in love.

○

CUT TO Therapist A: *A father-led discussion about male nudity*
*is catharsis that can let your son crack a hymen out of biological needs.*

○

CUT TO My secret adolescence weekends:
Cruising as posing, born of coincidence.

○

Secrets give a pleasure easy to improvise, like a script.

○

CUT TO Now: looping
the line *Could we start over?*
from the film doesn't make the wrench
between me & him excusable.

○

CUT TO Therapist B: *A wife isn't really a dagger that stops one from ribboning oneself.*

○

Still, how many lines can I cut or cut
to to really mean        start over.

# DARK ADAPTATION

Complete all blanks on the behalf of light. There isn't much it can do: it can't narrate a love story without drinking me down. Once, time carried me to a book, then a body, & I knew there was repulsion in both. It carried me to hands that made me present, like the now-ness of the news. Then it carried me to those who cast me away like a satellite. The space inside a shopping mall feels immortal. I smell the skin of twinks who mix cheap perfume samples with youth that works & wrecks.

# STRAIGHT CITY

If marriages are
about instinct, why

are my parents sad
watching me

intend to be
nothing? *Our family*

*tree is ruined.* Yet,
aren't fallen

leaves a loss
all trees take

in? This city
can't define

children. To me,
a choice (mine

to lose), or a ditch
(I've been told

to drink from). Where
I'll lick the city's

glans, a prattling
lily knot.

# WAR NOTES ON A GENRE CALLED "FATHER"

A ghost in me obnubilates my father's face. Its reluctance to collect any grainy dailiness when he was a child.

In most horror films, it's rare to see both parents simultaneously haunted or exorcising for their haunted child.

The genre's reluctance to break its convention is budget-related, meaning ghosts can also be poor.

What my father lacked was common as a knife, a sieve, or a storybook. Born when the Japanese occupied Hong Kong, he lost his sense of time.

A fictional origin: *July 15, 1946.* He could be older, balder, less pulverized, more prime.

Birth certificates were fabricated during the Japanese invasion. Wars manifest temporal chaos to national & individual histories. Lock survivors & survival in a disjuncture.

Baba. In *Babadook* (2014), when the clawed shadow popped up nightly from a storybook, the son had to act like he had lost it before the mother took the knife & held it in reproach by the kitchen sink.

She lost it, too. It is the genre's tendency to deceive & to deliver deception into a climax.

The son was her dinghy, a hero with a blanched face, reminding her not to act like a sieve.

Miró's *Hair Pursued by 2 Planets* (1968): an apple of acidic red pierced by a four-legged fork, soured. An eidetic shoe. Though the painting reflects massive destruction of war, the vibrancy of colors brings its objects to life.

But if objects are alive, we say they are cursed—like the bad book from *Babadook*.

*[Miró] explored certain themes such as that of* Mother and Child *repeatedly throughout his long career.*

In Urdu & Hindi, *babadook* means *father-grief.*

In real life, ghosts never gutturalize *Baba* before they appear. They are among us, common like a knife, a sieve, a storybook.

A beach with no sand is a haunting.

If there is a ghost in me, there is a living object in me. Me: half-me, half-object. But it is unfair to only blame the object-half for not knowing my father's past well.

After years of gazing at buttocks, a psychic told me that I was full of feminine energies.

*In classical Chinese literature, the female spectre [is] positioned as pure yin in relation to "man as the fullest flowering of yang," the ghost is a foil to human, as woman is to man.*

Once, in Barcelona, a tour guide said it's impossible to talk about the Spanish Civil War in an hour. So, he talked about—

*Bombing did not guarantee accuracy. Gravity, wind, & the pilot in the wind.*

People hid in shelters. Buckets of water. Ripples as forecast. Limbs to bandage. Some tore their husbands', fathers', or brothers' shirts into strips. The guide used *them* to mean *women*, without saying *women* in the first place.

I'm approximating my father. My eyes opening, though *the opening eye of horror is far more often an eye on the defense than an eye on the offense.*

My father was less impressed by Barcelona than Madrid, where he bought a Royal Madrid jersey with no name or number on its back.

The land lived through the Spanish Civil War. The coastline didn't.

Barcelona's cannons missed the bombing jets, explosives dived into the sea. Water is the best absorbent of failure.

When my father ran away from the bombing Japanese, did he look back? Or, before it happened, did his head practice turning with precision to witness the burning, the smoke of family trees?

He was too young to practice looking back to install memory.

He told me Grandpa died of a heart attack at home when a bomb fell. He said nothing of how Grandpa's body was found, how he reacted in the moment of fatherlessness.

How did he feel when the notion of Father started to dematerialize?

How to translate the smoothness of wounds without scratching them into words?

# OUTER POWER

On April 18, 1930, at 8:45pm, the BBC announced: "There is no news."


Inside every TV set, a crow
& moody dove are ready to mate.
No one could explain the snow then.
The fun part about memory
is that it's a seated hero, not necessarily
well-rested. It doesn't matter
how big or smart the TV is, be happy
with its longitudinal emptiness.
Bored by the news of email leaks,
I thought, *I'd be lucky to see someone
report this in runway hair.*
A message sits in my spam box:
a man sends me rotgut in an e-mug
he expects me to e-touch.
I want alternatives, especially when
I'm outside my psychiatrist's chair,
where I'm charged $600/face.
With that face, a landslide
of whispers. The bio-waste of whispering
causes hallucination, the news says—
& that politicians are layered like onions.
These politicians with their blowhole
mouths make us addicts of ache
when we watch the space open & shut.
Without a TV, my eyes go electron-bright.
A grackle pecks at them like they're sesame seeds.

# APOLOGIA OF THE BESIEGED CITY

Some people love like they believe the romantic

folklore about the moon, but they love too literally

from inside a spacesuit. Or they love to feel

like a shell put back onto the sand. They love

the shoreline, without loving to trudge

back up to hard land. They love sleeping over.

In the dark, they love grazing my chest with defeat.

Imagine the vibe in bed. Imagine how hard

it is for me to love them back. They're blind puppies

when we fuck. They wriggle around to find

an available nipple to nurse. They love dirty

talk. They love asking for permission to lash out.

They love doing it when I moan. They love to hear *Sure.*

They love me as much as they love the spasms inside electric

Tenga cups. They love bathing me afterward. It's pretty, they know.

Their terror lathering along my calves, so tangible & white.

# ACKNOWLEDGEMENTS

Poems in this manuscript have appeared in the following publications, with revision: *The Asia Literary Review, Asian-American Literary Review, Australian Book Review, Barn Owl Review, Bellingham Review, Copper Nickel, Diode, Griffith Review, Grist, Gulf Coast, The Margins, The Missouri Review Online, Of Zoos, Ostrich Review, The Poetry Review, SubLevel, Third Coast, Wasafiri,* and *Verse Daily.* These poems are also anthologized in *No News: 90 Poets Reflect on a Unique BBC Newscast* (Recent Work Press, 2020), *One Hand Clapping* (Guggenheim, 2018), *Silence* (The University of Canberra, 2019), and *The Queer Movement: Anthology of Literatures* (Seagull Books, 2021).

Thank you to Noemi Press and the entire team for making my voice heard.

Thank you to the University of Canberra Vice-Chancellor's International Poetry Prize, Poetry on the Move, Sing Lit Station, Singapore Writers Festival, The Hawker Prize for Southeast Asian Poetry, the Peter Porter Poetry Prize, the Guggenheim Foundation, the amazing team of Taipei Poetry Festival, and the Renaissance Foundation for their trust and encouragement.

Special thanks to my friends and literary culprits for lending me an ear when I much needed reassurance: Christopher Chien, Daryl Lim, Mary Jean Chan, Collier Nogues, James Shea, Li Mei Ting, Louise Law, Tang Siu Wa, Cheuk Wan Chi, Kyle Fung, Chester Wong, Edmond Tong, Francol Cheng, Albert Au Yeung, and many other social media friends.

Thank you to my family for their absolute tolerance of me. Thank you, John. Thank you, Bradley, whose paw I miss holding in bed. Thank you to Cantopop and Mandopop songs. Thank you to everyone who chose to stand with Hong Kong.

# NOTES

"First Martyr" was written in memory of a protestor who fell from a shopping mall podium after hanging banners demanding the Hong Kong Government to withdraw the Extradition Bill.

"Apology to a Besieged City" adopts language from Zbigniew Herbert's "Reports from the Besieged City."

Poems titled "Dark Adaptation" were commissioned by Solomon R. Guggenheim Museum, New York, as part of "Glitch: An Evening of Poetry and Catalogue Launch for *One Hand Clapping*." They were inspired by the homophonic translation of the following Cantopop songs: "Queen's Road East" (1991), "The Boundless Oceans, Vast Skies" (1993), and "Eggs and Lamb" (2014).

"101, Taipei" alludes to an essay from Mary Ruefle's *Madness, Rack, and Honey* (Wave Books, 2012).

"Nationalism Is a Tote Bag I Use Every Day" adopts language from Susan Glaspell's *Trifles* (1916).

"Five Acts with Father" is a juxtaposition of languages from Ghassan Zaqtan's *Like a Straw Bird It Follows Me* (Yale University Press, 2012) and a list from Jamie Keddie's *Images* (Oxford University Press, 2009).

"Golden" is written with multiple Cantonese Internet slangs popular in Hong Kong Internet forums.

> 001
> Agger: originally the last name of Daniel Agger, a Danish footballer from the Liverpool Football Club. Internet forum users adopted the word (by error at first, but with intention later) as a mutated form of *agree*. Goodest: an alternative, though ungrammatical, form of *best*, often used ironically to mock someone's low English proficiency.

> 002
> 煩膠: a term coined and commonly used on GOLDEN, often referring to mean or ill-intended acts to provoke or cause annoyance. The term literally means "annoying plastic" in Chinese.

## 003
認真就輸了: originally from a novella of the same title by a mainland Chinese author, in which characters use the phrase to describe transient romance.

## 004
回帶: an Internet term referring to the act of reposting old news as if it was new. The term literally means "rewind" in Chinese.

## 007
中出: originated in Japanese straight pornography, the term refers to the act of ejaculating inside the woman's body. It was later used by Internet forum users to mean irresponsible acts or decisions that cause trouble to others. Despite the term's sexual denotation, it has been used numerous times in Hong Kong's pro-China newspapers as an abbreviation of The Hong Kong Chinese Importers' & Exporters' Association. The term literally means "middle exit" in Chinese.

## 008
左膠: leftard. The term literally means "left plastic" in Chinese.

## 012
J: short for *jer*, which, in Cantonese, refers to the male penis. The alphabet's part of speech varies in its colloquial usage. It can be a verb, a noun, or an adjective. When used as a verb, it means "masturbating over (something/ someone)" or, metaphorically, "showing intense admiration toward (something/ someone)."
巴打: a Cantonese homophonic translation of the English word *brother*, which refers to male Internet forum users.

## 013
HTML: an abbreviation of How To Make Love.

## 014
hehe: a popular term on GOLDEN since 2013, referring to gay issues or individuals.
FF: short for *fantasy*; inspired by the video game *Final Fantasy*.

## 016
y已x: a unique GOLDEN syntactical form that subverts traditional use of Chinese subject-verb collocation, which adopts the xy-structure (where x is a verb and y is a noun). The Chinese word "已" literally means already.

## 019
啪啪啪: an onomatopoeia originally referring to applause, but was later adopted by Hong Kong Internet users as a metonymy for sexual intercourse.

"City Mess, Mother Mess, Fluids Mess" partially contains language of Mark Doty, Brenda Hillman, Adam Zagajewski, and Allan Kaprow.

"Invitation" was commissioned by Taipei Poetry Festival, and was written for Taipei City. Popular cultural references in the poem that may be foreign to American readers include: 唐綺陽 (nationally famous Taiwanese astrologist), 張君雅 (ambassador and symbol of a Taiwanese instant noodles brand of the same name), 阿妹 (famous Taiwanese female singer openly supportive of sexual minorities), 連名帶姓 (Mandarin song of A-Mei from her album *Story Thief*), 小李子 (traditional rice porridge shop in Taipei City), 仁愛路 (major arterial road in Taipei City, literally meaning a road of kindness and love).

"War Notes on a Genre Called Father" adopts language from Bliss Cua Lim's academic essay, "Spectral Times: The Ghost Film As Historical Allegory" (2001).

"Apologia of the Besieged City" adopts language from *Francis Ponge: Selected Poems* (Wake Forest University Press, 1994).

Nicholas Wong is the author of *Crevasse* (Kaya Press), the winner of the 2016 Lambda Literary Award for Gay Poetry. He is also the recipient of the 2018 Peter Porter Poetry Prize. Wong has contributed to the radio composition project "One of the Two Stories, or Both" at the Manchester International Festival, and the catalogue of the exhibition "One Hand Clapping" at the Guggenheim Museum.